World War Two Trivia Crossword

B N William

Thank you for your purchase

I hope you enjoy the book as much
as we did making it,
please consider leaving a
review on Amazon

As a small independent author
reviews really help other
people make informed
purchases.

Please Enjoy

PUBLISH

Join us on your favourite platform, Scan the QR code on your phone or tablet

Allies

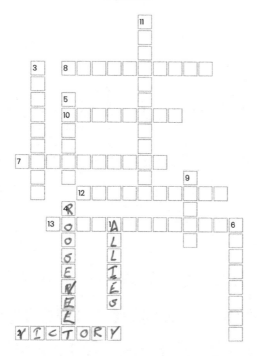

Across

[2] The ultimate goal of the Allies in World War II

[7] Supreme Allied Commander in Europe during D-Day

[8] The process of setting free from occupation

[10] Codename for the Allied invasion of Normandy

[12] Underground movements opposing Axis occupation

[13] Cooperation among Allied nations to achieve victory

Down

[1] Nations united against the Axis Powers

[3] British Prime Minister who led the Allies

[4] US President who supported the Allies

[5] Country that played a major role in the Allied victory

[6] Location of the D-Day invasion by the Allies

[9] The strength of the Allied nations working together

[11] Soldiers who landed by parachute behind enemy lines

Axis Powers

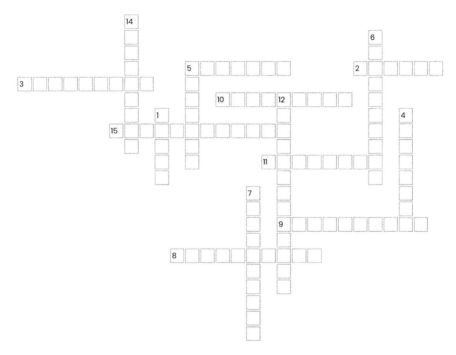

Across

[2] German dictator and leader of the Nazi Party

[3] Italian fascist dictator

[5] Political ideology embraced by the Axis Powers

[8] Control and administration of conquered territories

[9] The aggressive actions and policies of the Axis Powers

[10] Systematic genocide carried out by the Nazis

[11] Deliberate extermination of a specific group of people

[15] Form of government pursued by the Axis Powers

Down

[1] Alliance between Germany, Italy, and Japan"

[4] Emperor of Japan during World War II

[5] Adjective describing the ideology of the Axis Powers

[6] Lightning-fast warfare used by the Axis Powers

[7] Manipulative information spread by the Axis Powers

[12] Internment of targeted individuals in camps

[14] Axis Powers' goal of territorial conquest

D-Day

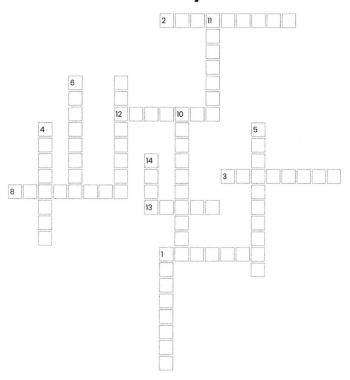

Across

[1] Codename for the naval component of the D-Day operation

[2] The Allied landings on June 6, 1944 "

[3] Utah, Omaha, Gold, Juno, and Sword "

[8] Floating harbors used to support the invasion

[12] The goal of the D-Day invasion was to restore freedom

[13] One of the D-Day landing beaches in Normandy

Down

[1] Region in France where the D-Day invasion took place

[4] Codename for the D-Day operation

[5] Supreme Commander of the Allied forces on D-Day

[6] Paratroopers who were dropped behind enemy lines

[10] Actions against the German occupation in France

[11] The successful outcome of the D-Day operation

[14] One of the D-Day landing beaches in Normandy

Battle of Stalingrad

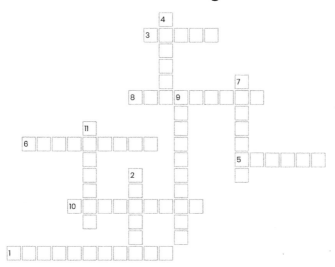

Across

[1] City in southwestern Russia, site of a major WWII battle *

[3] Prolonged military blockade during the Battle of Stalingrad

[5] Skilled marksman involved in urban warfare during the battle

[6] The Battle of Stalingrad resulted in heavy casualties

[8] German forces eventually capitulated in Stalingrad

[10] The battle was fought fiercely on the frontline positions

Down

[2] German leader who ordered the attack on Stalingrad

[4] Harsh weather conditions played a role in the battle's outcome

[7] Acts of bravery and valor during the Battle of Stalingrad

[9] The determination and resilience of Soviet soldiers

[11] The Soviet Union's ultimate triumph in Stalingrad

Pearl Harbor

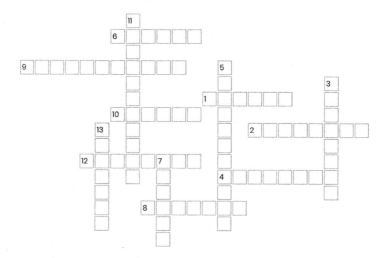

Across

[1] Location of the Pearl Harbor attack

[2] Nation responsible for the attack on Pearl Harbor

[4] The element of surprise in the attack

[6] The attack involved Japanese aerial bombardment

[8] Theater of war where Pearl Harbor is located

[9] Honoring the lives lost in the Pearl Harbor attack

[10] The naval base that was the primary target of the attack

[12] The USS Arizona Memorial commemorates the attack

Down

[3] Month when the attack on Pearl Harbor occurred

[5] USS Arizona, USS Oklahoma, and USS Missouri "

[7] President Roosevelt's description of the attack

[11] Pearl Harbor suffered significant destruction

[13] The attack on Pearl Harbor preceded the US entry into WWII

Blitzkrieg

Across

[3] Armored vehicles used in the Blitzkrieg offensives

[7] The force and intensity of Blitzkrieg attacks

[8] Quickly penetrating enemy lines in Blitzkrieg assaults

Down

[1] Lightning warfare used by the Axis Powers

[2] Country that employed the Blitzkrieg strategy

[4] German Air Force supporting the Blitzkrieg tactics

[5] Rapid movement and coordination characteristic of Blitzkrieg

[6] Catching the enemy off guard was a key element of Blitzkrieg

[9] British term for the German air raids during WWII

[10] The flexible movement and positioning in Blitzkrieg

Holocaust

Across

[1] Systematic genocide during World War II

[5] Imprisonment of targeted individuals in camps

[6] The process of setting free from occupation

[7] Site of the post-war trials of Nazi leaders

[8] Segregated areas where Jewish people were forced to live

[10] Manipulative information spread during the Holocaust

[11] Personal accounts and stories from Holocaust survivors

Down

[2] Infamous concentration camp in Poland

[3] Deliberate extermination of a specific group of people

[4] German political party responsible for the Holocaust

[9] Honoring and remembering the victims of the Holocaust

Atomic Bomb

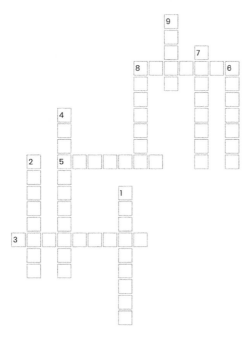

Across

[3] Harmful energy released by the atomic bomb

[5] Site of the first test of the atomic bomb in the US

[8] Nuclear reaction process

Down

[1] Japanese city targeted by the atomic bomb

[2] Second Japanese city hit by the atomic bomb

[4] Massive devastation caused by the atomic bomb

[6] Pertaining to the energy released by the atomic bomb

[7] Emperor of Japan during World War II

[8] Contaminated particles following the atomic bomb explosion

[9] Powerful explosion

Resistance Movements

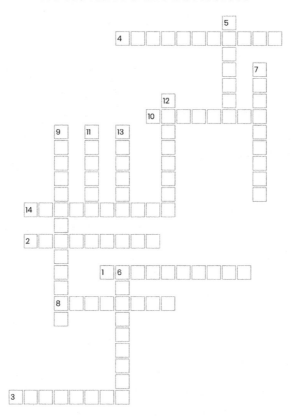

Across

[1] Underground movements against Axis occupation

[2] Fighters who opposed occupying forces

[3] Deliberate damage or disruption of enemy operations

[4] Secret networks supporting resistance efforts

[8] Areas under enemy control during World War II

[10] One who carries out acts of sabotage

[14] The ultimate goal of resistance movements

Down

[5] Bravery and determination shown by resistance fighters

[6] Gathering intelligence against the occupying forces

[7] Irregular warfare tactics used by resistance fighters

[9] Cooperation among resistance groups for a common cause

[11] Secret codes and encryption used by resistance fighters

[12] Another term for resistance fighter or partisan

[13] Uprising against the occupying forces

Evacuation

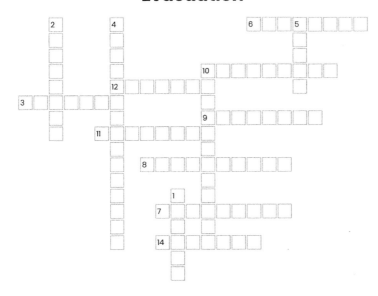

Across

[3] Place of refuge during bombings

[6] Luggage used by evacuees

[7] Control of limited resources during war

[8] Families torn apart during evacuation

[9] Challenge of establishing one's identity in a new place

[10] Welcome and support for evacuees

[11] Newcomers in the receiving areas

[12] Individual relocated for safety

[14] Joyous moment when families are reunited

Down

[1] Concern for well-being during wartime

[2] Displaced individuals seeking shelter

[4] Rescue effort for Jewish children

[5] Mode of transport for evacuations

[10] Process of documenting evacuees

Air Raids

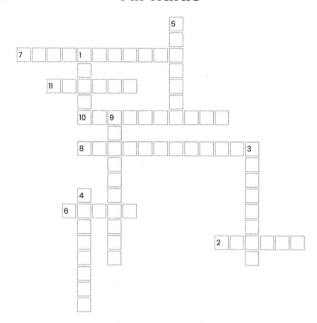

Across

[2] Warning signals of imminent bombings

[6] Intense and sustained bombing campaign

[7] Strategy to cause widespread fires

[8] Beams used to locate enemy aircraft

[10] Seeking protection during air raids

[11] Destruction caused by bombings

Down

[1] Explosive devices dropped from aircraft

[3] Protective structures during air raids

[4] Darkening of cities to hide from enemy aircraft

[5] Military aircraft used in air defense

[9] Relocation of civilians during air raids

Codebreaking

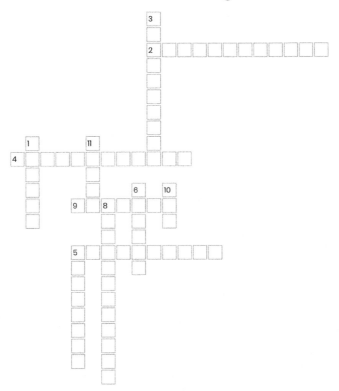

Across

[2] Study of secret codes and communication

[4] Gathering and analysis of secret information

[5] Encrypted or coded text

[9] Device used to assist in codebreaking

Down

[1] German encryption machine

[3] Process of decoding a message

[5] Reference book containing codes and their meanings

[6] Secret writing system or code

[8] Person skilled in codebreaking

[10] Information needed to decode a message

[11] Codename for intelligence obtained from decrypting Enigma messages

Women in War

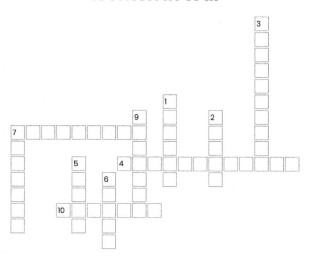

Across

[4] Women deciphering enemy codes and ciphers

[7] Women's contributions and losses in war

[10] Military woman

Down

[1] Women providing medical care on the battlefield

[2] Women gathering secret information for their side

[3] Women actively opposing the enemy occupation

[5] Women in aviation during wartime

[6] Recognition for exceptional service

[7] Women providing aid and assistance

[9] Courageous female fighter

Propaganda

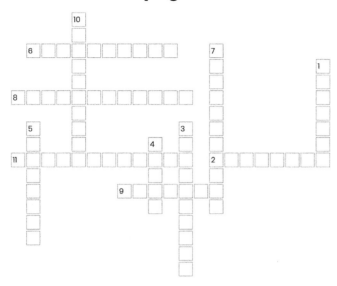

Across

[2] Printed materials distributed to spread specific ideas

[6] Love and support for one's country

[8] Individual responsible for creating and disseminating propaganda

[9] Visual representations used to evoke emotions and ideas

[11] Portrayal of an enemy as evil or threatening

Down

[1] Visual displays used to promote certain messages

[3] Control and restriction of information flow

[4] Movies designed to shape public opinion

[5] Public addresses intended to sway attitudes

[7] Strong identification and loyalty towards one's nation

[10] Act of convincing or influencing others

Espionage

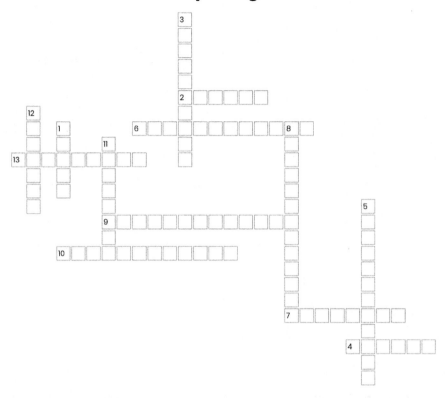

Across

[2] Secret or hidden operations

[4] Secret writing system or code

[6] Monitoring and observation of targets

[7] Deliberate destruction or disruption of enemy operations

[9] Questioning of suspects or captured spies

[10] Gathering and analysis of secret information

[13] System of allocating scarce resources to civilians

Down

[1] Individuals gathering secret information for their side

[3] Concealed identity for intelligence-gathering purposes

[5] Penetration of enemy territory or organization

[8] Study of codes and ciphers to decipher encrypted messages

[11] Altering one's appearance to avoid detection

[12] Acting in a secretive and inconspicuous manner

Rationing

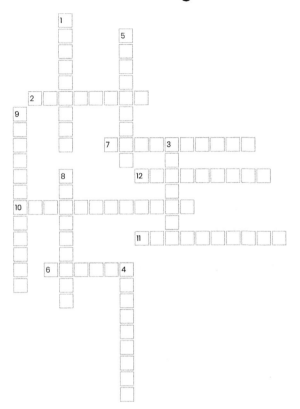

Across

[2] Limited availability of goods during wartime

[6] Imposed restrictions on consumption during wartime

[7] Distribution of resources based on need during wartime

[10] Preservation of resources for the war effort

[11] Controlled consumption of goods during wartime

[12] Thriftiness in resource usage during wartime

Down

[1] Control of limited resources during wartime

[3] Vouchers for limited supplies during wartime

[4] Giving up luxuries for the war effort

[5] Insufficient supply of goods during wartime

[8] Measures to conserve resources during wartime

[9] Guidelines for limited usage of goods during wartime

Victory Gardens

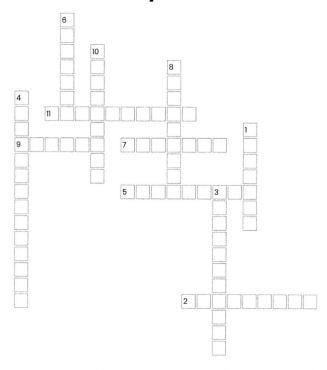

Across

[2] Collaboration in growing and sharing garden produce

[5] Plentiful harvest from personal gardens

[7] Distributing garden produce among neighbors and friends

[9] Flourishing growth of plants in personal gardens

[11] Edible plants cultivated in personal gardens

Down

[1] Homegrown produce from personal gardens

[3] Providing fresh and healthy food during shortages

[4] Growing food in an environmentally friendly way

[6] Fruits and vegetables grown in personal gardens

[8] Produce grown in one's own backyard

[10] People who cultivate their own gardens

War Bonds

Across

[1] Financial support for the war effort

[2] Supporting the country's war efforts

[5] Providing resources for the war through financial means

[7] Setting aside money for war bonds

[8] Love and loyalty for one's country during wartime

[11] People who organize events to collect funds for the war

Down

[3] Collecting money to support the war

[4] Financial instruments to support the war

[6] Donations and investments for the war effort

[9] Backing the war effort through financial means

[10] Individuals who contribute funds for war bonds

Manhattan Project

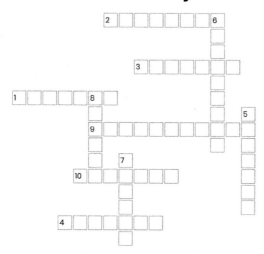

Across

[1] Relating to the use of atomic energy

[2] Scientific investigations during the project

[3] Process of splitting atomic nuclei

[4] Strict measures to keep the project confidential

[9] Prominent scientist involved

[10] The scientific research involved

Down

[5] Key element used in the development of the atomic bomb

[6] Japanese city where an atomic bomb was dropped

[7] Classified nature of the project

[8] Pertaining to atomic energy

Concentration Camps

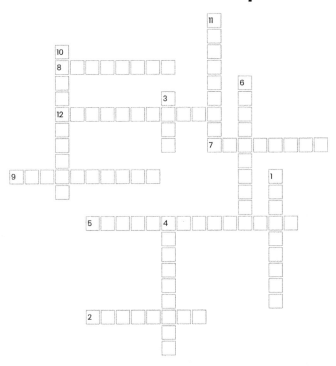

Across

[2] Deliberate extermination of a specific group of people

[5] Stripping of human dignity in concentration camps

[7] Individuals who managed to escape concentration camps

[8] Cruel and without compassion

[9] Horrific acts committed in concentration camps

[12] Commemoration of the victims of concentration camps

Down

[1] Systematic genocide during World War II

[3] German political party responsible for the concentration camps

[4] Infamous concentration and extermination camp in Poland

[6] Forced detention of individuals in concentration camps

[10] Freedom from captivity in concentration camps

[11] Individuals held against their will in concentration camps

Invasion of Normandy

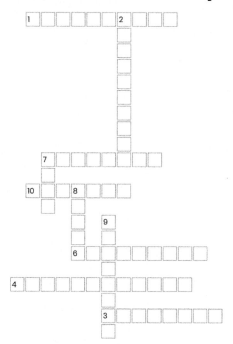

Across

[1] Landing zones established by the Allied forces

[3] Region in northern France where the invasion took place

[4] Soldiers dropped behind enemy lines on D-Day

[6] Planned military operation to gain a significant advantage

[10] Objective of the invasion

Down

[2] Supreme Allied Commander during the invasion

[7] Opposing forces

[8] Armored vehicles used in the invasion

[9] Paratroopers' role in the operation

Battle of Midway

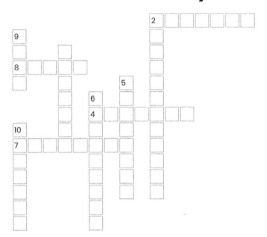

Across

[2] Aircraft carrier played a significant role in the battle

[4] Naval weapon used in the battle

[7] Key component in the air-sea battle

[8] Pertaining to the navy

Down

[2] Allied intelligence efforts to decipher Japanese codes

[5] U.S. aircraft carrier involved in the battle

[6] Battle with crucial implications for the war in the Pacific

[9] Month of the battle

[10] Ocean theater of the battle

Battle of the Bulge

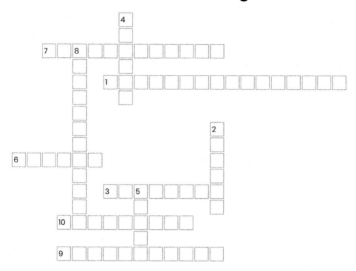

Across

[1] German attempt to turn the tide of the war

[3] Belgian town with a crucial role in the battle

[6] German armored units used in the offensive

[7] German initial success in penetrating Allied lines

[9] Area of active military operations

[10] Battle with significant implications for the outcome of the war

Down

[2] Harsh weather conditions during the battle

[4] American general known for his leadership during the battle

[5] German strategy to encircle and isolate Allied forces

[8] Allied forces surrounded by German troops

Nuremberg Trials

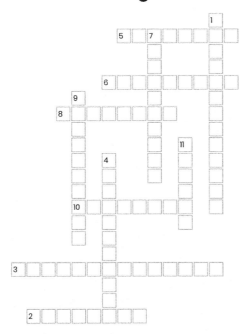

Across

[2] Court established to prosecute the accused

[3] Holding individuals responsible for their actions

[5] Verdicts rendered by the tribunal

[6] German city where the trials took place

[8] Deliberate extermination of a specific group of people

[10] Unprecedented international legal proceedings

Down

[1] Trials held with the participation of multiple nations

[4] Presentation of evidence against the defendants

[7] Individuals accused of war crimes and crimes against humanity

[9] High-ranking officials held accountable for their roles in the war

[11] Lasting impact of the Nuremberg Trials on international law

Hiroshima

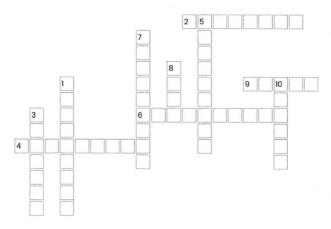

Across

[2] Commemorative site in Hiroshima

[4] Long-term health effects of the atomic bomb

[6] Efforts to reconstruct Hiroshima after the bombing

[9] Desire for peace after the event

Down

[1] Individuals who lived through the atomic bombing

[3] Enormous loss of life and destruction

[5] Massive blast that leveled buildings and structures

[7] Physical and emotional pain endured by the victims

[8] Atomic weapon used

[10] Month of the bombing

Nagasaki

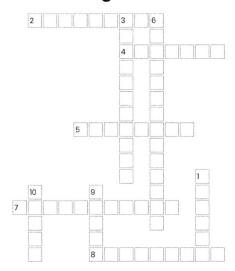

Across

[2] Japanese surrender following the atomic bombings

[4] People affected by the bombing and its aftermath

[5] Significant event marking the use of atomic weapons in warfare

[7] Extensive damage caused

[8] Individuals who lived through the event

Down

[1] Aircraft that delivered the atomic bomb

[3] Widespread destruction caused by the atomic bomb

[6] Efforts to rebuild Nagasaki after the bombing

[9] Resulting aftermath

[10] Desire for peace after the event

V-J Day

Across

[2] Japanese Emperor announces the end of the war

[3] Atomic bombing contributed to the Japanese surrender

[4] Japanese Emperor during the war

[7] Joyful celebration of the end of the war

[9] Freedom from occupation and oppression

[11] Remembrance of the sacrifices made during the war

Down

[1] Defeated nation in the Pacific

[5] Cessation of hostilities between Japan and the Allies

[6] Celebrating the end of the Pacific conflict

[8] Restoration of tranquility after the war

[10] Ceasefire agreement marking the end of hostilities

Lend-Lease Act

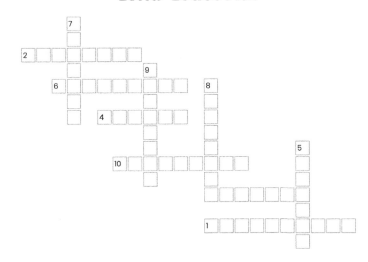

Across

[1] Providing aid to allies during the war

[2] Military equipment and goods sent to allied nations

[4] Nations receiving aid under the Lend-Lease Act

[6] Ensuring the efficient delivery of supplies to allies

[10] International cooperation facilitated by the act

Down

[5] Countries benefitting from Lend-Lease without taking sides

[7] Backing provided to allied nations

[8] Legislative body that passed the act

[9] Beneficiaries included armed forces

Tuskegee Airmen

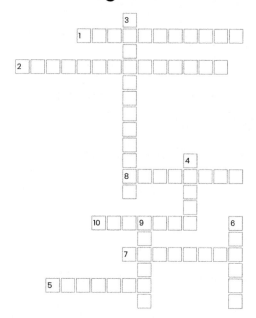

Across

[1] Struggle against racial discrimination in the military

[2] Facing prejudice and inequality in the military

[5] Dedicated commitment to their country during wartime

[7] Preparation for aerial combat

[8] Nickname of the Tuskegee Airmen

[10] Role as combat pilots

Down

[3] Pioneers breaking racial barriers in the military

[4] Demonstrating courage and bravery in combat

[6] Lasting impact on military and civil rights

[9] Recognized for their achievements

V-E Day

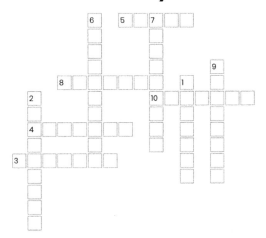

Across

[3] Defeated nation in Europe

[4] Joyful celebration of the end of the war in Europe

[5] Restoration of tranquility after the war

[8] Celebratory marches in cities across Europe

[10] Overcoming adversity and achieving victory

Down

[1] Celebrating the end of the European conflict

[2] Axis forces surrender to the Allies

[6] Freedom from occupation and oppression

[7] Ceasefire agreement marking the end of hostilities

[9] Remembrance of the sacrifices made during the war

Battle of Britain

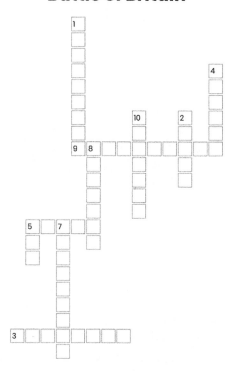

Across

[3] Iconic British fighter aircraft used in the battle

[5] Technological advantage aiding British defenses

[9] Operation to save civilians

Down

[1] German air force launching attacks on Britain

[2] Intense bombing campaign by the Germans

[4] Target of heavy bombings during the battle

[5] Royal Air Force

[7] Close-range aerial battles between fighter planes

[8] British resilience leads to victory in the battle

[10] Bravery displayed by the defenders

The Great Escape

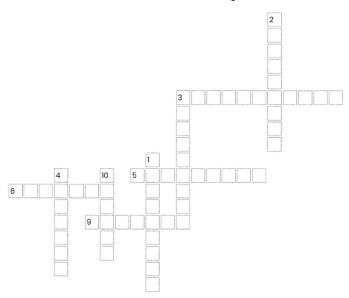

Across

[3] Secretive and covert activities involved in the escape

[5] Those who successfully evaded capture after the escape

[6] Brave actions of the escapees in the face of danger

[9] Creation of false documents

Down

[1] Digging tunnels to escape the camp

[1] Secret passage used

[2] Harsh punishments for those involved in the escape

[3] Condition of being held prisoner

[4] The ultimate goal of the escape attempt

[10] Those involved in the escape attempt

Warsaw Uprising

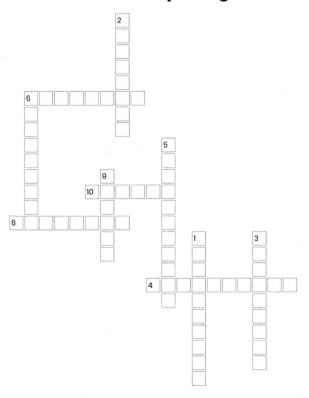

Across

[4] Unity among the Polish resistance fighters

[6] Uprising seen as a symbol of Polish resistance and defiance

[8] Commemorations honoring the participants of the uprising

[10] Uprising against occupying forces

Down

[1] Armed opposition against German occupation

[2] Massive rebellion against the German forces

[3] Ordinary people joining the fight against the Germans

[5] Heavy damage inflicted on Warsaw during the uprising

[6] Many lives lost in the fight for freedom

[9] Lasting impact of the Warsaw Uprising on Polish history

Code Talkers

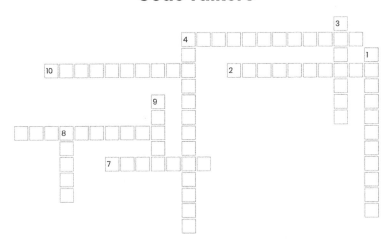

Across

[2] Process of encoding messages to protect their content

[4] Code talker activities kept strictly confidential

[7] Confidentiality of the coded messages

[10] Process of decoding enemy messages

Down

[1] Code talker messages considered secure and undecipherable

[3] Branch of the military where many code talkers served

[4] Code talkers' significant contribution to the war

[8] Technology used for transmitting messages

[9] Recognition for their contributions

War Correspondents

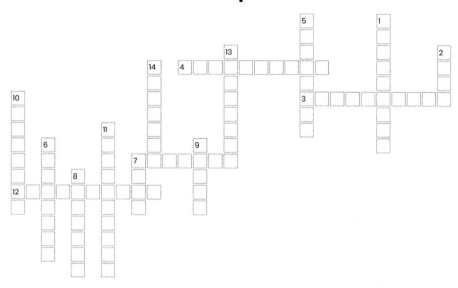

Across

[3] Reports and articles sent from war correspondents

[4] Areas of conflict and direct engagement in the war

[7] Detailed accounts of events and developments in the war

[12] Seeing and reporting events as they unfold

Down

[1] Journalists providing news coverage from the frontlines

[2] Information and updates from the war zones

[5] Journalists living and working with military units

[6] News stories and reports about the war

[7] Dangers faced by war correspondents in combat zones

[8] Observers documenting events and sharing firsthand accounts

[9] Media organizations responsible for reporting news

[10] Providing knowledge and insight into the war

[11] Profession focused on gathering and reporting news

[13] Deep understanding of the conflict through reporting

[14] Bravery displayed by war correspondents in dangerous situations

War Artists

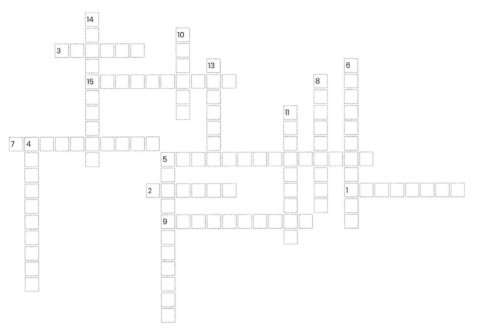

Across

[1] Expressing the war experience through artistic creations

[2] Surface for painting war scenes and experiences

[3] Artworks that convey messages and emotions through images

[5] Artistic perspectives on the war and its effects

[7] Artistic representations that prompt contemplation and thought

[9] Depicting scenes and events through drawings and paintings

[15] Documenting and preserving the history of war through art

Down

[4] Using art to communicate thoughts and feelings about the war

[5] Creative interpretations of the war through artistic vision

[6] Honoring the sacrifices and experiences of those involved in the war

[8] Three-dimensional artworks representing war themes

[10] Materials and techniques used by war artists

[11] Engaging viewers with compelling and impactful artworks

[13] Areas of conflict depicted in the artworks

[14] Artistic choices that evoke emotional responses

Home Guard

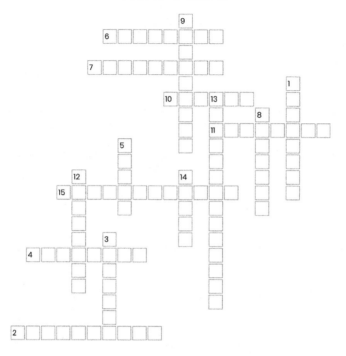

Across

[2] Citizens who offer their services to protect their country

[4] People taking an active role in protecting their communities

[6] Organizing and preparing for defense in times of war

[7] Collective effort to safeguard the home front

[10] Monitoring and protecting specific areas within the community

[11] Measures taken to ensure safety and protection

[15] Readiness to respond to any threats or emergencies

Down

[1] Non-military individuals serving in a defense role

[3] Guarding against potential threats on the home front

[5] Guarding and securing specific areas within the home country

[8] Providing assistance and resources to the military and defense efforts

[9] Maintaining constant watchfulness for any signs of danger

[12] Equipping civilians with necessary skills for defense roles

[13] Recognizing the duty to protect and serve the home front

[14] Coming together as a community to defend common interests

Battle of Guadalcanal

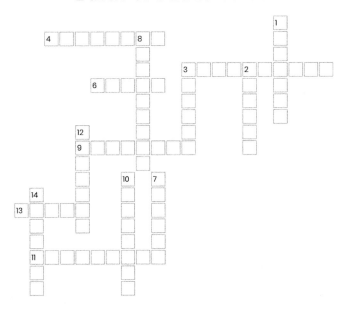

Across

[3] Combining land and sea operations in the battle

[4] Opposing forces during the Battle of Guadalcanal

[6] Involvement of naval vessels and naval warfare

[9] Control of the airfield on Guadalcanal was a key objective

[11] Allied forces launching an offensive against the Japanese

[13] Prolonged engagement and efforts to hold ground

Down

[1] Theater of war where the battle took place

[2] Geographic location of the battle in the Solomon Islands

[3] Collective forces fighting against the Japanese

[7] Dense vegetation and challenging terrain on the island

[8] Significance of the battle in the overall war effort

[10] Battle for control of critical supplies and resources

[12] US Marine Corps playing a major role in the battle

[14] Allied forces ultimately secured victory in the battle

Battle of Iwo Jima

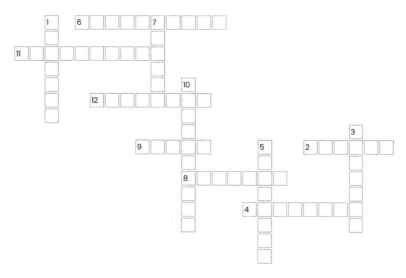

Across

[2] Geographic location of the battle in the Pacific Ocean

[4] Opposing forces during the Battle of Iwo Jima

[6] Combining land and sea operations in the battle

[8] Elaborate network of underground tunnels and caves on the island

[9] Involvement of naval vessels and naval gunfire support

[11] Iwo Jima served as a strategic base for the Allied forces

[12] Commemorations honoring the sacrifices made during the battle

Down

[1] Theater of war where the battle took place

[3] US Marine Corps played a major role in the battle

[5] Island terrain characterized by volcanic ash and rugged landscape

[7] Fortified underground positions used by Japanese defenders

[10] Heavy losses suffered by both sides during the battle

Resistance Fighters

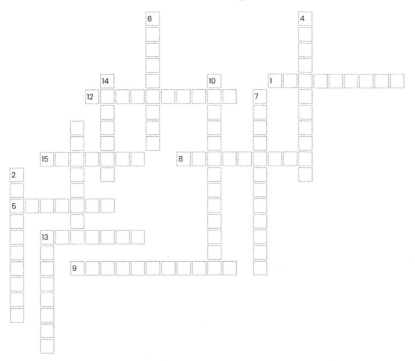

Across

[1] Irregular forces engaged in resistance activities

[5] Bravery displayed by resistance fighters in the face of danger

[8] Armed uprising against occupying forces

[9] Secretive and covert activities involved in the resistance

[12] Undermining the enemy's control and authority

[13] Operating discreetly to avoid detection and capture

[15] Fighting for freedom and liberation from occupation

Down

[2] Resistance against enemy forces in occupied territories

[4] Operating clandestinely to avoid detection by the enemy

[6] Individuals carrying out acts of sabotage against the enemy

[7] Secretly penetrating enemy lines to gather intelligence

[10] Cooperation among resistance groups and local communities

[13] Destroying or disabling enemy infrastructure and equipment

[14] Providing assistance to resistance fighters and their cause

Operation Market Garden

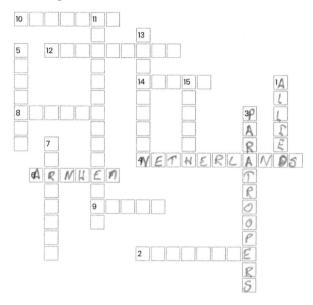

Partially filled crossword grid with answers:
- 4 Across: NETHERLANDS
- 6 Across: ARNHEM
- Down (1): ALLIED (vertical, right side)
- Down (3): PARATROOPERS (vertical, right side)

Across

[2] Involvement of airborne forces in the operation

[4] Geographic location of the operation in Dutch territory

[6] Strategic target and site of fierce fighting during the operation

[8] Aircraft used to transport troops and supplies during the operation

[9] Armored vehicles supporting the ground forces during the operation

[10] Operation Market Garden did not achieve its overall objectives

[12] Complex planning and coordination of supplies and support

[14] Challenges and setbacks that hindered the operation's progress

Down

[1] Collective forces undertaking the operation

[3] Elite soldiers dropped behind enemy lines during the operation

[5] Key objectives of the operation were to secure bridges

[7] Establishing a supply route through enemy-held territory

[11] Efforts to provide additional troops and resources

[13] City captured by Allied forces during the operation

[15] Enemy resistance and counterattacks encountered during the operation

Battle of Kursk

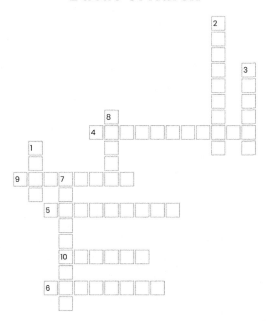

Across

[4] Major tank battle and focal point of the battle

[5] Significance of the battle in the overall war effort

[6] Defensive fortifications dug by both sides

[9] Foot soldiers engaged in close combat during the battle

[10] Heavy casualties suffered by both

Down

[1] Armored vehicles played a major role in the battle

[2] Soviet forces established defensive positions against the Germans

[3] Opposing forces during the Battle of Kursk

[7] Heavy guns and artillery bombardments in the battle

[8] Tanks and armored vehicles used by both sides

Battle of Berlin

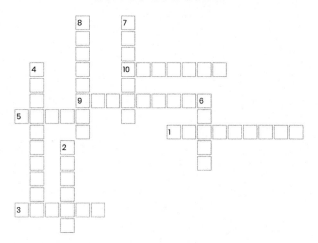

Across

[1] Symbolic building captured by Soviet forces during the battle

[3] Final German surrender and end of World War II in Europe

[5] Prolonged blockade and assault on the city

[9] German capitulation at the end of the battle

[10] Significance of the Allied victory

Down

[2] Adolf Hitler's last refuge in Berlin

[4] Last-ditch German resistance against the advancing Soviet forces

[6] Widespread destruction and devastation in Berlin

[7] Soviet forces secure victory and the end of Nazi Germany

[8] German fortifications in Berlin

Victory in Europe

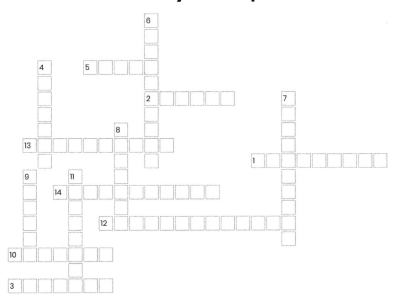

Across

[1] German surrender marking the end of the war in Europe

[2] Collective forces celebrating victory in Europe

[3] German capital captured, symbolizing victory in Europe"

[5] Restoration of peace after years of war

[10] Reconstruction and rebuilding efforts in war-torn Europe

[12] German surrender without any conditions or terms

[13] Allied forces occupying Germany after the war

[14] Reflecting on the significance of the victory and its impact

Down

[4] Celebrations and joyous scenes across Europe

[6] Freedom from German occupation in Europe

[7] British Prime Minister during the war, instrumental in victory"

[8] US President at the end of the war, involved in post-war planning"

[9] Victory parades held in major cities across Europe

[11] Commemorations honoring the victory and those who sacrificed

Victory in the Pacific

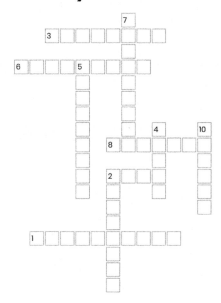

Across

[1] City devastated by the atomic bomb, hastening Japanese surrender"

[2] Role of naval forces

[3] Japanese suicide pilots making desperate attacks against Allied ships

[6] Cessation of hostilities and declaration of peace in the Pacific

[8] Emotional response to victory

Down

[2] Second city targeted by the atomic bomb

[4] Japanese capital targeted by strategic bombing raids

[5] Long and grueling Pacific campaigns and battles

[7] Honoring the sacrifices made by servicemen and civilians during the war

[10] Feeling of liberation after the war

Allied Leaders

Across

[1] US President during most of World War II

[2] British Prime Minister and one of the key Allied leaders

[4] US President in the final stages of the war

[5] Supreme Commander of the Allied Expeditionary Forces in Europe

[7] Prominent military leaders and strategists within the Allied forces

[9] US general known for his leadership in the European theater

[11] Allied leaders working together in a unified front

Down

[3] Leader of the Soviet Union during the war

[6] British general and key figure in the European theater

[7] US general involved in the Pacific theater

[8] Soviet general and prominent military leader

[12] Collaborative planning and decision-making by Allied leaders

Axis Leaders

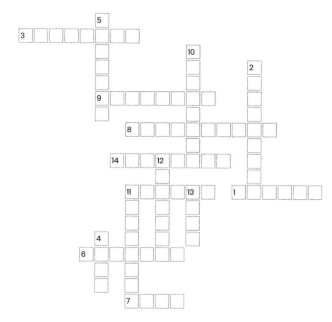

Across

[1] German dictator responsible for the Holocaust

[3] Emperor of Japan during the war

[6] German Nazi leader and key figure in the Holocaust

[7] Hitler's deputy and prominent Nazi official

[8] Nazi foreign minister involved in war crimes

[9] German SS officer responsible for organizing the Holocaust

[11] Japanese diplomat involved in war crimes

[14] Nazi propaganda minister

Down

[2] Italian fascist leader during World War II

[4] Japanese general and Prime Minister during the war

[5] SS leader involved in Nazi war crimes

[10] Infamous Nazi doctor known as the ""Angel of Death"" "

[11] High-ranking SS officer and key architect of the Holocaust

[12] Nazi official and Hitler's private secretary

[13] Japanese general and Prime Minister during the war

War Crimes

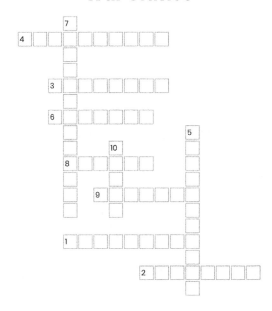

Across

[1] Systematic genocide of Jews and others by the Nazis

[2] Deliberate extermination of a specific group

[3] Brutal killing of a large number of people

[4] Horrific acts of violence or cruelty

[6] Infliction of severe physical or psychological pain

[8] Legal proceedings for accountability

[9] Pursuit of fair treatment

Down

[5] Systematic mistreatment or harassment of a group

[7] Cooperation with the enemy during wartime

[10] International court for war crimes

PUBLISH

Join us on your favourite platform, Scan the QR code on your phone or tablet

Allies

[1↓] Allies
[2→] Victory
[3↓] Churchill
[4↓] Roosevelt
[5↓] Soviet
[6↓] Normandy
[7→] Eisenhower
[8→] Liberation
[9↓] Unity
[10→] Overlord
[11↓] Paratroopers
[12→] Resistance
[13→] Collaboration

Axis Powers

[1↓] "axis
[2→] Hitler
[3→] Mussolini
[4↓] Hirohito
[5→] Fascism
[5↓] Fascist
[6↓] Blitzkrieg
[7↓] Propaganda
[8→] Occupation
[9→] Aggression
[10→] Holocaust
[11→] Genocide
[12↓] Concentration
[14↓] Expansion
[15→] Totalitarian

D-Day

[1↓] Normandy
[1→] Neptune
[2→] "invasion
[3→] "beaches
[4↓] Overlord
[5↓] Eisenhower
[6↓] Airborne
[8→] Mulberry
[8→] Mulberry
[10↓] Resistance
[11↓] Victory
[12→] Liberty
[13→] Omaha
[14↓] Juno

Battle of Stalingrad

[1→] "stalingrad
[2↓] Hitler
[3→] Siege
[4↓] Winter
[5→] Sniper
[6→] Sacrifice
[7↓] Heroism
[8→] Surrender
[9↓] Resilience
[10→] Frontline
[11↓] Victory

Pearl Harbor

[1→] Hawaii
[2→] Japanese
[3↓] December
[4→] Surprise
[5↓] "battleship
[6→] Aerial
[7↓] Infamy
[8→] Pacific
[9→] Remembrance
[10→] Harbor
[11↓] Devastation
[12→] Memorial
[13↓] Prelude

Blitzkrieg

[1↓] Blitzkrieg
[2↓] Germany
[3→] Tanks
[4↓] Luftwaffe
[5↓] Speed
[6↓] Surprise
[7→] Overwhelming
[8→] Breakthrough
[9↓] Blitz
[10↓] Maneuver

Holocaust

[1→] Holocaust
[2↓] Auschwitz
[3↓] Genocide
[4↓] Nazi
[5→] Concentration
[6→] Liberation
[7→] Nuremberg
[8→] Ghettos
[9↓] Remembrance
[10→] Propaganda
[11→] Testimony

Atomic Bomb

[1↓] Hiroshima
[2↓] Nagasaki
[3→] Radiation
[4↓] Destruction
[5→] Trinity
[6↓] Nuclear
[7↓] Hirohito
[8↓] Fallout
[8→] Fission
[9↓] Blast

Resistance Movements

[1→] Resistance
[2→] Partisans
[3→] Sabotage
[4→] Underground
[5↓] Courage
[6↓] Espionage
[7↓] Guerrilla
[8→] Occupied
[9↓] Collaboration
[10→] Saboteur
[11↓] Cipher
[12↓] Partizan
[13↓] Revolt
[14→] Liberation

Evacuation

[1↓] Safety
[2↓] Refugees
[3→] Shelter
[4↓] Kindertransport
[5↓] Train
[6→] Suitcase
[7→] Rationing
[8→] Separation
[9→] Identity
[10→] Reception
[10↓] Registration
[11→] Arrivals
[12→] Evacuee
[14→] Reunion

Air Raids

[1↓] Bombs
[2→] Sirens
[3↓] Shelters
[4↓] Blackout
[5↓] Fighter
[6→] Blitz
[7→] Firebombing
[8→] Searchlights
[9↓] Evacuation
[10→] Sheltering
[11→] Damage

Codebreaking

[1↓] Enigma
[2→] Cryptography
[3↓] Decryption
[4→] Intelligence
[5→] Ciphertext
[5↓] Codebook
[6↓] Cipher
[8↓] Cryptanalyst
[9→] Machine
[10↓] Key
[11↓] Ultra

Women in War

[1↓] Nurses
[2↓] Spies
[3↓] Resistance
[4→] Codebreakers
[5↓] Pilot
[6↓] Medal
[7↓] Support
[7→] Sacrifice
[9↓] Heroine
[10→] Soldier

Propaganda

[1↓] Posters
[2→] Leaflets
[3↓] Censorship
[4↓] Films
[5↓] Speeches
[6→] Patriotism
[7↓] Nationalism
[8→] Propagandist
[9→] Symbols
[10↓] Persuasion
[11→] Demonization

Espionage

[1↓] Spies
[2→] Covert
[3↓] Undercover
[4→] Cipher
[5↓] Infiltration
[6→] Surveillance
[7→] Sabotage
[8↓] Cryptanalysis
[9→] Interrogation
[10→] Intelligence
[11↓] Disguise
[12↓] Stealth
[13→] Rationing

Rationing

[1↓] Shortages
[2→] Scarcity
[3↓] Coupons
[4↓] Sacrifice
[5↓] Shortfall
[6→] Limits
[7→] Allocation
[8↓] Austerity
[9↓] Restrictions
[10→] Conservation
[11→] Restrained
[12→] Frugality

Victory Gardens

[1↓] Harvest
[2→] Community
[3↓] Nourishment
[4↓] Sustainability
[5→] Abundance
[6↓] Produce
[7→] Sharing
[8↓] Homegrown
[9→] Thrive
[10↓] Gardeners
[11→] Vegetables

War Bonds

[1→] Investment
[2→] Patriotic
[3↓] Fundraising
[4↓] Bonds
[5→] Funding
[6↓] Contributions
[7→] Savings
[8→] Patriotism
[9↓] Support
[10↓] Investors
[11→] Fundraisers

Manhattan Project

[1→] Nuclear
[2→] Research
[3→] Fission
[4→] Secrecy
[5↓] Uranium
[6↓] Hiroshima
[7↓] Secret
[8↓] Atomic
[9→] Oppenheimer
[10→] Science

Concentration Camps

[1↓] Holocaust
[2→] Genocide
[3↓] Nazi
[4↓] Auschwitz
[5→] Dehumanization
[6↓] Internment
[7→] Survivor
[8→] Inhumane
[9→] Atrocities
[10↓] Liberation
[11↓] Prisoners
[12→] Remembrance

Invasion of Normandy

[1→] Beachheads
[2↓] Eisenhower
[3→] Normandy
[4→] Paratroopers
[6→] Strategic
[7↓] Axis
[8↓] Tanks
[9↓] Airborne
[9↓] Airborne
[10→] Victory

Battle of Midway

[2→] Carrier
[2↓] Codebreaking
[4→] Torpedo
[5↓] Yorktown
[6↓] Strategic
[7→] Aircraft
[8→] Naval
[9↓] June
[10↓] Pacific
[10↓] Pacific

Battle of the Bulge

[1→] Counteroffensive
[2↓] Winter
[3→] Bastogne
[4↓] Patton
[5↓] Siege
[6→] Panzer
[7→] Breakthrough
[8↓] Encirclement
[9→] Battlefront
[10→] Strategic

Nuremberg Trials

[1↓] International
[2→] Tribunal
[3→] Accountability
[4↓] Prosecution
[5→] Judgment
[6→] Nuremberg
[7↓] Defendants
[8→] Genocide
[9↓] Leadership
[10→] Historic
[11↓] Legacy

Hiroshima

[1↓] Survivors
[2→] Memorial
[3↓] Tragedy
[4→] Radiation
[5↓] Explosion
[6→] Rebuilding
[7↓] Suffering
[8↓] Bomb
[9→] Peace
[10↓] August

Nagasaki

[1↓] Bomber
[2→] Surrender
[3↓] Devastation
[4→] Victims
[5→] Historic
[6↓] Reconstruction
[7→] Destruction
[8→] Survivors
[9↓] Ruins
[10↓] Peace

V-J Day

[1↓] Japan
[2→] Surrender
[3→] Nagasaki
[4→] Hirohito
[5↓] Ceasefire
[6↓] Victory
[7→] Rejoice
[8↓] Peace
[9→] Liberation
[10↓] Armistice
[11→] Memorial

Lend-Lease Act

[1→] Assistance
[2→] Supplies
[4→] Allies
[5↓] Neutral
[6→] Logistics
[7↓] Support
[7↓] Support
[8↓] Congress
[9↓] Military
[10→] Agreement

Tuskegee Airmen

[1→] Segregation
[2→] Discrimination
[3↓] Trailblazers
[4↓] Valor
[5→] Service
[6↓] Legacy
[7→] Training
[8→] Redtails
[9↓] Heroes
[10→] Fighter

V-E Day

[1↓] Victory
[2↓] Surrender
[3→] Germany
[4→] Rejoice
[5→] Peace
[6↓] Liberation
[7↓] Armistice
[8→] Parades
[9↓] Memorial
[10→] Triumph

Battle of Britain

[1↓] Luftwaffe
[2↓] Blitz
[3→] Spitfire
[4↓] London
[5↓] Raf
[5→] Radar
[7↓] Dogfights
[8↓] Victory
[9→] Evacuation
[10↓] Courage

The Great Escape

[1↓] Tunneling
[1↓] Tunnel
[2↓] Reprisals
[3→] Clandestine
[3↓] Captivity
[4↓] Freedom
[5→] Survivors
[6→] Courage
[9→] Forgery
[10↓] Heroes

Warsaw Uprising

[1↓] Resistance
[2↓] Uprising
[3↓] Civilians
[4→] Solidarity
[5↓] Destruction
[6→] Symbolic
[6↓] Sacrifice
[8→] Memorial
[9↓] Legacy
[10→] Revolt

Code Talkers

[1↓] Unbreakable
[2→] Encryption
[3↓] Marines
[4→] Confidential
[4↓] Contributions
[7→] Secrets
[8↓] Radio
[9↓] Honor
[10→] Decryption
[10→] Decryption

War Correspondents

1↓] Reporters
2↓] News
3→] Dispatches
4→] Frontlines
5↓] Embedded
6↓] Coverage
7↓] Risk
7→] Reports
8↓] Witness
9↓] Press
10↓] Informed
11↓] Journalism
12→] Eyewitness
13↓] Insights
14↓] Courage

War Artists

1→] Artistic
2→] Canvas
3→] Visual
4↓] Expression
5↓] Imagination
5→] Interpretation
6↓] Commemorate
7→] Reflection
8↓] Sculpture
9→] Illustrate
10↓] Medium
11↓] Captivate
13↓] Warzone
14↓] Aesthetics
15→] Historical

Home Guard

[1↓] Civilian
[2→] Volunteers
[3↓] Defense
[4→] Citizens
[5↓] Local
[6→] Mobilize
[7→] Community
[8↓] Support
[9↓] Vigilance
[10→] Patrol
[11→] Security
[12↓] Training
[13↓] Responsibility
[14↓] Unity
[15→] Preparedness

Battle of Guadalcanal

[1↓] Pacific
[2↓] Island
[3→] Amphibious
[3↓] Allied
[4→] Japanese
[6→] Naval
[7↓] Jungle
[8↓] Strategic
[9→] Airfield
[10↓] Supplies
[11→] Offensive
[12↓] Marines
[13→] Siege
[14↓] Victory

Battle of Iwo Jima

[1↓] Pacific
[2→] Island
[3↓] Marines
[4→] Japanese
[5↓] Volcanic
[6→] Amphibious
[7↓] Bunker
[8→] Tunnels
[9→] Naval
[10↓] Casualties
[11→] Occupation
[12→] Memorial

Resistance Fighters

[1→] Partisans
[2↓] Occupation
[4↓] Underground
[5→] Courage
[6↓] Saboteurs
[7↓] Infiltration
[8→] Rebellion
[9→] Clandestine
[10↓] Collaboration
[12→] Subversion
[13↓] Sabotage
[13→] Stealth
[13↓] Sabotage
[14↓] Support
[15→] Liberty

Operation Market Garden

[1↓] Allied
[2→] Airborne
[3↓] Paratroopers
[4→] Netherlands
[5↓] Bridges
[6→] Arnhem
[7↓] Corridor
[8→] Glider
[9→] Tanks
[10→] Failure
[11↓] Reinforcements
[12→] Logistics
[13↓] Eindhoven
[14→] Delay
[15↓] Ambush

Battle of Kursk

[1↓] Tank
[2↓] Defensive
[3↓] German
[4→] Prokhorovka
[5→] Strategic
[6→] Trenches
[7↓] Artillery
[8↓] Armor
[9→] Infantry
[10→] Losses

Battle of Berlin

[1→] Reichstag
[2↓] Bunker
[3→] Defeat
[4↓] Resistance
[5→] Siege
[6↓] Ruins
[7↓] Victory
[8↓] Defenses
[9→] Surrender
[10→] Triumph

Victory in Europe

[1→] Surrender
[2→] Allies
[3→] "berlin
[4↓] Rejoice
[5→] Peace
[6↓] Liberation
[7↓] "churchill
[8↓] "truman
[9↓] Parade
[10→] Rebuild
[11↓] Memorial
[12→] Unconditional
[13→] Occupation
[14→] Remembrance

Victory in the Pacific

[1→] "hiroshima
[2↓] Nagasaki
[2→] Navy
[3→] Kamikaze
[4↓] Tokyo
[5↓] Endurance
[6→] Ceasefire
[7↓] Sacrifice
[8→] Rejoice
[10↓] Relief

Allied Leaders

[1→] Roosevelt
[2→] Churchill
[3↓] Stalin
[4→] Truman
[5→] Eisenhower
[6↓] Montgomery
[7↓] Macarthur
[7→] Marshal
[8↓] Zhukov
[9→] Patton
[11→] Coalition
[12↓] Strategy

Axis Leaders

1→] Hitler
2↓] Mussolini
3→] Hirohito
4↓] Tojo
5↓] Himmler
6→] Goering
7→] Hess
8→] Ribbentrop
9→] Eichmann
10↓] "mengele
11↓] Heydrich
11→] Hirota
12↓] Bormann
13↓] Tōjō
14→] Goebbels

War Crimes

1→] Holocaust
2→] Genocide
3→] Massacre
4→] Atrocities
5↓] Persecution
6→] Torture
7↓] Collaboration
8→] Trials
9→] Justice
10↓] Hague

Thank you

Please review

B N William

Printed in Great Britain
by Amazon

28351542R00046